CONTENTS

THE ITALIAN CHRISTMAS COOKBOOK

Mariam Trolle

&

Jeanett Weiss

PREFACE OF THE PUBLISHER

We are pleased that you have chosen this book.
If you are in possession of a paperback book, we will gladly send you the same as an e-book, then you can easily turn the pages digitally as well as normally.

We attach great importance to the fact that all of our authors, when creating their own cookbooks, have recooked all of their recipes several times.
Therefore, the quality of the design of the recipes and the instructions for recooking are detailed and will certainly succeed.

Our authors strive to optimize your recipes, but tastes are and will always be different!

We at Mindful Publishing support the creation of the books, so that the creative authors of the recipes can take their time and enjoy cooking.

We appreciate your opinion about our recipes, so we would appreciate your review of the book and your experience with these great recipes!

In order to reduce the printing costs of our books and to offer the possibility to offer recipes in books at all, we have to do without pictures in the cookbooks. The digital version has the same content as the paperback.

Our recipes will convince you and reveal to you a culinary

style you can't get enough of!

TUSCAN NUT CAKE

Total time approx.: 45 minutes

Ingredients

100 g|Almond(s)
100 g|Hazelnuts
100 g|Walnuts
200 g|Apricot(s), dried
100 g|Orangeate
1 teaspoon|cinnamon powder
1 teaspoon|coriander
1 teaspoon|ginger powder
100 g|honey (acacia)
150 g|powdered sugar
2 tablespoons|flour
|butter, for the mould
|icing sugar, for sprinkling
|Cinnamon powder, for sprinkling

Preparation

Blanch and skin the almonds. Dry roast the hazelnut kernels in a pan until the skins start to crack. Put them in a kitchen towel that is as rough as possible and rub them until the skins come off. Dry roast the almonds, hazelnuts and walnuts, cool and chop coarsely. Dice the apricots very finely and mix well with the candied orange peel, nuts and spices. Melt the honey and icing sugar over a bain-marie while stirring constantly, allow to cool slightly and mix with the nut mixture. Sprinkle the flour over the mixture and knead well. Thinly butter a shallow pie dish, line it with baking paper and butter this as well. Spread the mixture evenly and press down firmly. Bake in a preheated oven at 130° C for 30 minutes. Leave to cool and dust thinly with icing sugar and a little cinnamon.

CANNARICULI

Total time approx.: 40 minutes

Ingredients

400 g|flour
100 g|sugar
1|lemon(s), of which the zest
⅛ litre|wine, white
2 tablespoons|marsala
1|egg(s)
1|egg(s), of which the yolk
1 pinch(s) of salt
|oil, for frying
200 g|honey

Preparation

Knead all the ingredients, except the honey, into a not too soft dough, adding a little flour if necessary. Cover the dough and let it rest for 30 minutes. Shape the dough into pencil-thick sticks about 5 cm long and deep-fry in plenty of hot oil. Drain the sticks on kitchen paper and place them on a plate that is not too flat. Heat the honey with a little water and pour over the cannariculi. Serve warm. Info: Cannariculi are traditionally served at Christmas in Calabria.

ALMOND SLICES

Total time approx.: 3 hours

Ingredients

125 g|Honey, liquid
75 g|Sugar
50 g|margarine
225 g|flour
½ packet|baking powder
2 teaspoons|cinnamon
½ teaspoon|gingerbread spice
|orange zest, grated from 2 oranges
300 g|marzipan - raw paste
1 medium|egg white
|flour

Preparation

Heat the honey with the sugar and margarine while stirring until the sugar has dissolved. Leave to cool. Mix the flour and baking powder, sift through. Knead into the honey mixture with the cinnamon and gingerbread spice and the grated zest of 1 orange. Cover the dough and leave to rest for 1 hour. Knead the marzipan with the remaining orange zest. Shape into 5 rolls about 20 cm long and chill the rolls for 45 minutes. Roll out the dough on a floured work surface to a rectangle of approx. 40 x 20 cm. Cut into 5 strips. Brush each strip with egg white and place a marzipan roll in the centre of each. Cover with pastry, pressing firmly at the seams. Place the rolls with the seam facing down on cling film and cover and chill, preferably overnight. The next day, cut into slices about 1.5 cm thick, place on baking paper with a little space between them and bake in a preheated oven at 180°C for about 15 minutes.

BISCUITS, ITALIAN

Total time approx.: 1 hour

Ingredients

4|egg(s), of which the white(s)
350 g|Almond(s), peeled, ground
200 g|Sugar
1 packet|vanilla sugar (Bourbon)
1 packet|flavouring (Finesse fine lemon zest)
150 g|Pine kernels
|powdered sugar

Preparation

Beat the egg whites until stiff, mix 200 g almonds, sugar, vanilla sugar and lemon zest, fold in, heat the mixture in a non-stick pan over low heat, stirring constantly, until it is reduced by half. Leave to cool. Stir in up to 100 g ground almonds, depending on the moisture. Dust your hands with icing sugar, form 1 teaspoon of dough into croissants. Place on a baking tray lined with baking paper. Bake in a preheated oven at 180°C on the middle shelf for 10 - 12 minutes.

ANISEED BREAD

Total time approx.: 45 minutes

Ingredients

350 g|flour
250 g|Butter
400 g|Almond(s), ground
125 g|Sugar
2 pack|vanillin sugar
1 teaspoon|lemon zest, grated
4|egg yolks
1 pinch(s)|salt
4 tablespoons|white wine
40 g|aniseed
400 g|powdered sugar
1|egg white

Preparation

Knead flour, butter, almonds, sugar, vanilla sugar, lemon zest, white wine, egg yolk and aniseed. Roll out the dough and cut out the biscuits. Bake for 10 - 15 minutes at 175°C. Beat the egg whites until stiff and stir in the icing sugar. Coat the hot biscuits with the mixture.

MORSETTI DI NATALE

Total time approx.: 7 days 1 hour 5 minutes

Ingredients

1 kg|flour
2 pack|baking powder
4|nutmeg
4|Lemon(s), organic, the zest of it
4|Tangerine(s), organic, the rind of it
4|Orange(s), organic, the rind thereof
330 g|Almond(s), ground
330 g|Hazelnuts, ground
330 g|Walnuts, ground
750 g|Sugar
2|egg(s)
100 g|Butter, room temperature
200 ml|milk
1 pinch(s) of salt

Preparation

Grate the 4 (!) nutmegs. Finely grate the peel of the citrus fruits. Then knead all the ingredients into a tough dough. Now form 3cm thick dough rolls on a floured surface and place them on a baking tray with baking paper. Bake in a preheated oven at 180 degrees for about 30 minutes. After baking, immediately cut diagonally into finger-thick slices and bake for another 10 minutes (similar to Cantuccini). Once cooled, store in a tin and leave to infuse for at least another week.

SOUP VENETIAN STYLE

Total time approx.: 30 minutes

Ingredients

2|Chicken thighs
2|Chicken breasts
250 g|beef, (breast core)
250 g|veal, (breast)
1|onion(s)
2|carrot(s)
1 small|celery
1 sprig/s|rosemary
2 tablespoons|olive oil
2|clove(s)
½ glass|wine, white, dry
50 g|butter fat
|salt
4 slice/s|toast bread
|Parmesan, grated

Preparation

Bring the chicken legs, beef and veal to the boil with the onion, carrots, quartered celery root and cloves in 1.5 litres of water. Cut the chicken breasts into small cubes and fry them in olive oil and butter together with the rosemary sprig. Deglaze with the white wine and cook on a high heat for about 5 minutes. Add to the stock. Continue to cook for approx. 3/4 hours. Remove the beef, veal and chicken legs from the broth and set aside (the fried chicken cubes remain as a garnish). Remove the vegetables from the broth. Place the toasted slices of bread in warmed plates, sprinkle with cheese and pour on the hot soup. You can use the rest of the meat to make a meat salad for the evening.

CHESTNUT PUDDING

Total time approx.: 1 hour 20 minutes

Ingredients

1 kg|Marone(s), (sweet chestnuts)
150 ml|milk, fresh whole milk (3.8% fat)
250 g|Sugar
1|vanilla pod(s)
40 g|cocoa powder
40 ml|Rum, brown (54%)
300 ml|cream, fresh
2 teaspoons|vanilla sugar
4 tablespoons|chocolate, shaved white

Preparation

Boil the chestnuts for about 50 minutes in a little water and peel them while still hot (also remove the inner thin skin). In the meantime, mix the milk with the scraped-out vanilla pulp, the scraped-out pod, the sugar and the cocoa and bring to the boil. Remove from the heat, remove the vanilla pod, add the rum. Press the chestnuts through a potato press, mix the chestnut puree and milk mixture. Divide the mixture between 4 dessert plates and again slowly press through the potato press. The result should be a tower like a spaghetti ice cream. Whip the cream with the vanilla sugar until stiff and place in dots around the chestnut pudding. Sprinkle a tablespoon of shaved white chocolate on each portion.

NUT - GINGER - CANTUCCINI

Total time approx.: 30 minutes

Ingredients

500 g|Wheat flour
250 g|Sugar, brown
2 teaspoon(s)|ginger, ground
1 pinch(s)|salt
1 teaspoon|baking powder
3 tablespoons|water, cold
3|egg(s) (size L)
100 g|butter or margarine
200 g|nuts (pecan nuts)
|grease for the baking tray

Preparation

Mix the flour, sugar, ginger, salt and baking powder together well, sifting if necessary. Add 3 tablespoons of cold water and knead together with the eggs and butter until smooth. Halve the pecans lengthwise and mix into the dough as well. Form rolls with a diameter of approx. 2-3 cm from the dough. Place on a greased baking tray and bake in a preheated oven at approx. 150-175 degrees for approx. 30 minutes. Remove the rolls from the oven, leave to cool for about 10 minutes and very carefully cut into slices of about 1 cm. Place the slices back on the tray and bake again at 175-200 degrees for about 15 minutes. After baking, remove the Cantuccini from the tray and leave to cool well.

ITALIAN PINE NUT BALLS

Total time approx.: 30 minutes

Ingredients

250 g|flour
1 teaspoon|dry yeast
2 pinches|salt
75 ml|Sherry, (Medium Dry)
75 ml|olive oil
100 g|sugar
100 g|Apple slices, dried (soft apple slices)
100 g|Pine nuts
|powdered sugar

Preparation

Cut the dried apple slices (preferably soft apple slices) into very small cubes. Put the flour, dry yeast and salt in a bowl. Add the olive oil and sherry and mix together. Now knead in the sugar, dried and diced apple pieces and pine nuts. Preheat the oven to 160°C (fan oven 140°C). Shape the dough into walnut-sized balls and place them on a baking tray lined with baking paper. Bake the pine nut balls for 15-20 minutes until light brown and crispy. Leave to cool on a cooling rack and sprinkle with icing sugar.

PANGANI

Total time approx.: 12 hours 30 minutes

Ingredients

300 g|Butter
350 g|Sugar, brown (farin sugar)
1 packet|vanilla sugar
1 teaspoon|cinnamon
1 pinch|cardamom
1|egg(s)
5 tablespoons|milk
750 g|flour
300 g|coating, for decorating

Preparation

Beat the butter with the sugar, vanilla sugar, cinnamon and cardamom until fluffy. Beat the egg over it and sift in the flour. Gradually knead with the milk until a firm dough forms. Shape the dough into about 4 rolls of about 3 cm diameter, then flatten the edges of the rolls so that you can cut squares from them. Place the rolls on a plate and chill overnight. Then cut approx. 6 mm thick slices from them and place on a prepared baking tray. Bake at 190°C for 12-15 min until light yellow. This will take about 3-4 trays. Melt the couverture and dip one corner of each pangani into the couverture. Wipe off the underside and let them dry on baking paper. They are not as crumbly and soft as most Christmas biscuits, but the taste and smell are really something.

CHRISTMAS CANTUCCINI

Total time approx.: 2 hours

Ingredients

260 g|flour
1 teaspoon|baking powder
180 g|sugar
1 package|vanilla sugar
½ teaspoon|gingerbread spice
1 pinch(s)|salt
40 g|marzipan paste, (finely diced)
25 g|Butter, soft
2|egg(s)
90 g|hazelnuts, (peeled/skinless)
90 g|Almond(s), (peeled/skinless)

Preparation

Mix all the ingredients, except the nuts, with the dough hook of a hand mixer or food processor until smooth. Knead in the shelled nuts. Divide the dough into four equal pieces and form each into 35 cm long rolls. Wrap in plastic wrap and chill for 1 hour. Then place the dough rolls 8 cm apart on a baking tray lined with baking paper. Pre-bake in the preheated oven at 200°C (fan oven 180°C) on the 2nd rack from the bottom for 15 minutes. Leave to cool and cut diagonally into 1 cm thick slices. Place the cut side of the Cantuccini on the baking tray and bake for another 8-10 minutes until golden brown.

PANETTONE

Total time approx.: 2 hours 45 minutes

Ingredients

150 g|Soft butter
80 g|Sugar
½ teaspoon|salt
4 medium|egg(s)
600 g|flour (type 405)
60 g|yeast, fresh
225 ml|water, lukewarm
190 g|raisins
45 g|Orangeate
45 g|lemon peel
1|vanilla pod(s), the pith thereof
1 teaspoon|lemon zest, untreated, grated
|butter for brushing
|flour for the work surface

Preparation

Prepare the baking paper for the clay pot (approx. 20 cm diameter) and set aside. Pour boiling water over the pot, preferably in a bucket, and leave it in the water. First test the empty clay pot to see if it will fit in the oven. If necessary, pull out the rack and place a cake rack on the bottom of the oven instead. Wash the sultanas, soak in hot water, drain and pat dry. Sift the flour into a large bowl and make a well in the centre. Crumble the yeast into the well, add a little warm water and stir with a little flour to form a so-called pre-dough. Cover with a cloth and leave to rise for about 15 minutes. In the meantime, separate the eggs and scrape out the pulp of the vanilla pod. Beat the egg yolks, sugar and vanilla pulp with the whisk of a hand mixer until a light cream is formed. Add the egg mixture, water and butter alternately to the flour and knead with the dough hooks until smooth. Cover again with the cloth and leave to rise for 1 1/2 hours. Preheat the oven (200°C top/bottom heat, hot air: 175°C, gas:level 3). Remove the clay pot from the water and line with the prepared baking paper. Place the dough on the floured work surface. Knead the sultanas, candied orange and lemon peel and grated lemon zest into the dough by hand. Pour into the clay pot and brush the surface with melted butter. Place in the oven and bake for about 20 minutes, then reduce the heat to 175°C (top/bottom heat, hot air: 150° C, gas: level 2) and bake for a further 60 minutes. If the surface gets too dark, cover with aluminium foil. When the baking time is up, remove the clay pot and place on a cooling rack. After five minutes, lift the cake out using the baking paper so that it does not get moist. Leave to cool on the cake rack. Then carefully remove the baking paper.

SIENA ALMOND BISCUITS

Total time approx.: 12 hours 30 minutes

Ingredients

250 g|Almond(s), peeled
150 g|Sugar
100 g|powdered sugar, (icing sugar)
1 packet|vanilla sugar, bourbon
2|egg(s), (of which the egg white for snow)

Preparation

Toast the almonds in a pan without fat, turning them repeatedly, then grind them finely. Mix the ground almonds with the sugar, half the icing sugar and the vanilla sugar. Beat the egg whites until very stiff and gradually fold in the almond mixture. Place the mixture on wrapping paper and carefully roll out and cut into rhombs, dust thickly with icing sugar and leave to rest overnight (12 hours), covered, in a cool place. Then heat the oven to 160° and bake for about 20 minutes. Leave to cool on a cooling rack and dust with icing sugar.

SPAGHETTI - COOKIES

Total time approx.: 30 minutes

Ingredients

125 g|flour
1 pinch|baking powder
50 g|sugar
1 pinch(s) salt
1|egg yolk
80 g|butter
350 g|marzipan paste
1 tablespoon|powdered sugar
1|egg white
6 tablespoons|jam, raspberry or strawberry jam
2 tablespoons|water
30 g|chocolate, white

Preparation

For the dough, mix the flour and baking powder. Add sugar, salt, egg yolk and butter and knead everything. Then divide into four parts and roll a sausage (about 5 cm in diameter) from each. Wrap each dough sausage in foil and chill for at least 30 minutes. Mix the marzipan, icing sugar and egg white until smooth and chill. Cut the dough rolls into finger-width slices, flatten and place on a baking tray lined with baking paper. Pre-bake the biscuits for 5 minutes at 180°C (top/bottom heat) or 160°C (fan oven). Put the marzipan mixture on the warm biscuits by pressing it through a garlic press onto the individual biscuits. While doing so, wipe off with the back of a damp knife. Bake the biscuits again at the same oven setting for 5-7 minutes. Let the biscuits cool and in the meantime warm the jam with the water and drizzle a little of it on each biscuit. Then just grate the white chocolate over the jam or alternatively melt and spread over the jam.

CHRISTMAS CANTUCCI

Total time approx.: 1 hour 30 minutes

Ingredients

250 g|flour
170 g|Almond(s), whole, unpeeled
190 g|Sugar
1 teaspoon|baking powder
1|vanilla pod(s)
25 g|Butter, soft
2|egg(s)
1 tablespoon|rum, brown
½ teaspoon|cinnamon
2 pinch|cardamom
1 pinch|star anise, ground
1 pinch(s)|clove(s), ground
1 pinch(s)|salt

Preparation

Put the almonds in a pot of boiling water for about 1 minute. Then drain and press the almonds out of the brown skins. Scrape the pulp out of the vanilla pod. In a bowl, mix the flour, baking powder, sugar, vanilla pulp, cardamom, cinnamon, star anise, cloves and 1 pinch of salt. Now add the soft butter, eggs and brown rum and knead very quickly with a mixer. Knead in the almonds and form the dough into a ball, wrap in cling film and chill for about 30 minutes. Cover the baking tray with baking paper and preheat the oven (top/bottom heat) to 190 degrees. After chilling, divide the dough ball into 6 pieces. Shape each piece of dough into a roll about 25 cm long. Place the dough rolls on the baking tray with a larger distance between them. The rolls will separate greatly. Pre-bake on the middle shelf for 15-20 minutes. Let the pastry cool a little and cut it diagonally with a serrated knife into slices about 1 cm thick. Place the cut side of the cantucci back on the baking tray and bake again at 180°C for 8-10 minutes until golden brown. Allow the Christmas cantucci to cool completely and place in a tin to store.

ITALIAN BISCOTTI

Total time approx.: 1 hour 45 minutes

Ingredients

250 g|flour
1 teaspoon|baking powder
75 g|sugar
1 packet|vanillin sugar
1 pinch(s) salt
1|egg(s), (size M)
1 teaspoon|aniseed, painted
75 g|butter
50 g|whipped cream
150 g|powdered sugar
2 tablespoons|maraschino
2 tablespoons|sugar - pearls, coloured

Preparation

Knead flour, baking powder, sugar, vanilla sugar, salt, egg, aniseed, fat and whipped cream with the dough hook of the hand mixer until smooth. Cover and chill for approx. 30 minutes. Roll out the dough into a rectangle (approx. 40 by 18 cm) and cut into strips (approx. 1.5 by 18 cm). Carefully loop each strip into a knot. Place on a baking tray lined with baking paper. Bake in a preheated oven at 200°C for about 15 minutes. Leave the biscuits to cool. Mix the icing sugar and liqueur, brush the biscuits with it and sprinkle with pearls.

CAPPUCCINO - LIQUEUR

Total time approx.: 30 minutes

Ingredients

2 teaspoons|coffee powder (espresso powder, Nescafe')
3 tablespoons|coffee powder (cappuccino powder)
10|egg yolk
1|egg white
1|vanilla pod(s), the pith
100 g|sugar
100 g|cream
¼ litre|rum, white

Preparation

Pour 3 tablespoons of boiling water over the espresso and cappuccino powder and stir. Beat the egg yolks and the fresh egg white, pulp from the vanilla pod and sugar in a bain-marie for about 10 minutes (it should become thick). Then slowly pour in the coffee mixture, cream and rum. If necessary, then strain and bottle.

FESTIVE MARINATED VENISON LEG

Total time approx.: 12 hours 30 minutes

Ingredients

1.2 kg|leg(s) of venison, boneless
2 stalk(s) of celery
500 ml|vinegar (wine vinegar)
3|Clove(s) of garlic
3|clove(s) of cloves
1 pinch(s)|cinnamon
1 teaspoon|rosemary
6|pepper - grains
80 g|butter
2|onion(s)
200 ml|Marsala
125 ml|vegetable stock
|salt
|pepper, black, from the mill

Preparation

Place the venison leg in a large freezer bag to marinate. Now make the marinade: Clean and roughly dice the celery. Add the vinegar, peeled garlic, cloves, cinnamon, rosemary, salt and peppercorns to the venison leg in the bag. Then seal the bag tightly and leave the whole thing to marinate overnight in the fridge. The next day, remove the leg of venison, drain well and pat dry. Peel and finely dice the onions. Heat the butter in a roasting tin and fry the diced onions and the marinade vegetables in it. Add the meat and fry until brown. Then salt and pepper it and pour Marsala and the vegetable stock over it. Cover and braise in a preheated oven at 120°C for about 150 minutes - if necessary, leave to marinate for a few more minutes in the switched-off oven. Then remove the legs and cut into slices. Strain the stock, season to taste and serve with the meat. Serve with Schupfnudeln, dumplings or spaetzle.

CHIANTI ROAST WITH TOMATOES

Total time approx.: 3 days 3 hours 30 minutes

Ingredients

2 kg|roast beef (shoulder)
2|carrot(s)
3 stalk/s|celery
2 stalk/s|leek
3|clove(s) of garlic, pressed
4 grains|allspice
1 teaspoon|peppercorns
3 sprig/s|rosemary
|thyme, a few sprigs
3|leafs of bay leaves, bent, fresh
750 ml|wine, (Chianti)
70 ml|Aceto balsamico, good quality
1 piece(s)|bacon rind
4 tablespoons|olive oil
|salt and pepper
1 tin|tomato(s), chopped
4|tomato(s), fresh, seeded, skinned, diced
3 teaspoons|sugar
3 tablespoons|tomato paste
|salt, (fleur de sel) to taste

Preparation

Coarsely dice the soup vegetables. Finely dice shallots and garlic.

Place the spice seeds in a tea filter and seal. Tie the herb sprigs into a bunch with the bay leaf. Place the prepared ingredients and meat in a large freezer bag, add the wine and vinegar, seal the bag and leave the meat to marinate in the refrigerator for 2-3 days. Turn in between. On the day of preparation, remove the meat from the marinade and dab dry. Pour the marinade through a sieve. Drain the vegetables well. Heat a roasting tin and rub with bacon rind. Add two to three tablespoons of oil and heat. Salt the meat and fry it well in the hot fat together with the rind. Remove the meat and the rind. Pour away the oil from browning. Heat the remaining oil in the roasting tin, add the drained marinated vegetables together with the spice bag and bouquet of herbs to the meat and roast everything vigorously. Sprinkle with sugar and let it caramelise slightly. Stir in the tomato purée and fry briefly. Add the canned tomatoes, salt and pepper. Pour in the marinade and bring to the boil. Preheat the oven to 160°. Place the meat in the sauce, cover and leave to braise in the oven for about one hour at 160°, one hour at 140° and one hour at 120°. Take out the meat, pass the sauce through a whisk. Simmer to taste, add the fresh tomato cubes, season with salt, pepper and aceto. Slice the meat, season with fleur de sel and serve with the sauce. Serve with a mashed potato, flavoured with garlic or even truffle butter to taste. A mash made of equal parts of celery and potatoes also tastes good with it. Before cutting, the roast must rest on a board covered with aluminium foil for 15 minutes.

VERMICELLI - CHESTNUT RICE

Total time approx.: 30 minutes

Ingredients

500 g|Chestnut(s)
250 ml|milk (I use 0.5 - 1.5%)
50 g|honey or icing sugar
1|vanilla pod(s), pith or 1 teaspoon vanilla powder
2 tablespoons|cognac or rum
250 ml|sweet cream
125 ml|chocolate sauce

Preparation

Boil cross-cut chestnuts covered with water in about 3/4 hours until soft, drain and peel. Puree with milk. Mix with honey or icing sugar, vanilla, rum and leave to cool. Whip cream until stiff, divide in the middle of 4 large dessert plates. Press the cold chestnut mixture like spaghetti ice cream through a potato or spätzles press or through a sieve with very large holes onto the cream. Serve with chocolate sauce.

TERLANO WINE SOUP

Total time approx.: 30 minutes

Ingredients

1|onion(s), finely chopped
500 ml|Broth (chicken, beef, vegetables...according to taste)
500 ml|wine, white
|salt and pepper
2|Yolk
⅛ litre|cream
|white bread
some|cinnamon

Preparation

Sauté the onion in a little butter, pour in the stock and white wine, season, simmer until the onions are nice and soft (puree afterwards if necessary). Stir the egg yolks with the cream and thicken the soup with it. CAUTION: do not let it boil any more, otherwise the egg will flocculate. Season to taste, make croutons from the white bread, sprinkle lightly with cinnamon. Serve the soup sprinkled with croutons!

BLOOD ORANGE PARFAIT

Total time approx.: 6 hours 30 minutes

Ingredients

5|Orange(s) (blood oranges)
4|egg(s)
60 g|Almond(s), sliced
100 g|Sugar
3 pack|vanilla sugar
½ litre|cream
1 tablespoon|orange liqueur
|fruit, to taste (e.g. raspberries frozen)
|Fruit and mint or lemon balm for decoration

Preparation

Toast the almond flakes without fat in a pan. Beat 4 egg yolks, sugar and 3 tablespoons hot water until creamy. Add 1 pinch of salt 1/4 litre blood orange juice (4 - 5 oranges) gradually. Whip the cream with vanilla sugar until stiff and stir into the cream with a whisk. Add 1 - 2 tablespoons of orange liqueur, mix in toasted almonds and fruit. Pour the mixture into a mould (a gugelhupf mould works well) and freeze in the freezer for approx. 6 hours. (Can also be prepared days in advance!) Remove from freezer 1/2 hour before serving. Place the mould briefly in hot water, carefully loosen the rim with a knife and turn out onto a plate. Garnish with orange slices and lemon balm.

WHITE TRUFFLES
WITH PASTA

Total time approx.: 10 minutes

Ingredients

250 g|Pasta (fettuccine, durum wheat)
|Salt water
4 tablespoons|butter flakes
1 pinch(s)|salt and pepper, white from the mill
1|truffle (white alba truffle)

Preparation

Cook the fettuccine in plenty of salted water until al dente. Drain the pasta and put it into a preheated pot. Sprinkle with butter flakes (not too little) and mix gently with the pasta. Add a little salt and very little pepper and mix. Serve on warmed plates and then slice the truffle, which has been cleaned beforehand, very thinly over the top. The recipe is simple and quick to prepare. Do not experiment and do not try to cook in a sophisticated way. The preparations are only for flavouring and as a "filling garnish". The star is the truffle, you should choose your accompaniment carefully and not season it too much.

NERO AND POLO

Total time approx.: 1 hour

Ingredients

250 g|Butter
150 g|Powdered sugar
250 g|flour
40 g|cocoa powder
2|Yolk(s)
1|egg(s)
1 pinch(s) salt
1 pinch(s)|vanilla
|jam, to taste
|cake icing, (chocolate icing)

Preparation

Cream butter with sugar, cocoa, salt and vanilla. Gradually beat in the yolks and the whole egg. Finally, beat in the flour. Using a piping bag and a medium smooth tube, pipe round, oval and biscuit shapes onto baking paper. Bake at approx. 210°C for 5 - 7 minutes. Remove from paper, assemble with jam and half dip in chocolate icing. You can also leave out the cocoa for a lighter version. I like to use apricot or strawberry jam.

ORANGE AMARETTI

Total time approx.: 1 hour 15 minutes

Ingredients

200 g|Powdered sugar
250 g|Almond(s), ground without skin
2|egg whites
½|Orange(s), grated peel
4 drops|bitter almond flavouring
45|flakes, (40 mm)

Preparation

Sift the icing sugar into a bowl. Add the almonds, egg whites, orange zest and bitter almond oil and mix well. Line 2 baking trays with baking paper and place the wafers on them. Shape the dough into balls, pressing the tip in a little, and place on the wafers. Leave the biscuits to dry for about 30 minutes. In the meantime, preheat the oven to 175°C. Bake for 15-20 minutes. Bake for 15-20 minutes. Store the cooled biscuits in tins.

CANTUCCINI

Total time approx.: 1 hour 30 minutes

Ingredients

175 g|Almond(s), whole
250 g|flour
180 g|Sugar
1 packet|baking powder
2 pack|vanilla sugar
½ bottle|bitter almond flavouring
3 tablespoons|butter
2|egg(s)
|salt

Preparation

Pour hot water over almonds and skin (best done the day before)
Prepare a kneaded dough from all ingredients. Add the almonds
at the end. Form the dough into a lump and chill for 60 minutes.
Divide the dough into six equal parts and form dough rolls
about 25cm long. Bake the dough rolls at 200 degrees in the
oven (preheated!) for 10-15 minutes. Cut the pre-baked dough
rolls into slices about 1 cm thick. Bake these slices (placed on the
cut surface) again in the oven at 200 degrees for 8-10 minutes.
The Cantuccini are ready! A nice gift at Christmas time.

PIGNOLI

Total time approx.: 27 minutes

Ingredients

200 g|Marzipan
115 g|Sugar
2|egg whites
5 tablespoons|flour
1 bag/s|vanilla sugar
100 g|Pine kernels
|powdered sugar for dusting

Preparation

Mix the sugar and marzipan in a food processor. Add the egg whites and vanilla sugar and mix again. Coarsely chop 30 g pine nuts in a freezer bag. Mix the chopped pine nuts and flour with the marzipan mixture. Using a tablespoon, cut off portions of the dough, place on a baking tray lined with baking paper, sprinkle with pine nuts and press them down a little. Bake the biscuits in the preheated oven at 180 °C (top/bottom heat) for 12 - 14 minutes, not too dark. Leave the pignoli to cool and dust with icing sugar.

BRUTTI MA BUONI

Total time approx.: 54 minutes

Ingredients

450 g|Nuts (hazelnuts, almonds or mixed nuts)
450 g|Sugar
150 g|egg white
1|vanilla pod(s)
1|lemon(s), the zest of it
|cinnamon

Preparation

Chop the nuts medium fine. Toast them in a fat-free pan with the cinnamon until they begin to smell fragrant. Beat the egg whites with a pinch of salt until foamy, gradually add the sugar until you have a white cream. Add the lemon zest and the vanilla pulp and beat again briefly. Put the nuts and the egg white cream in a saucepan, mix together and heat to approx. 40°C. Allow to cool slightly. The consistency should be like minced meat mixture. Preheat the cooker to 150 - 160 degrees. Now place small heaps (not too big) on the baking tray with the help of 2 teaspoons. Bake for 20 - 24 minutes.

MINI-PANETTONE

Total time approx.: 2 hours 40 minutes

Ingredients

50 ml|milk
8 g|Vanilla sugar
15 g|Fresh yeast
1 pinch(s) salt
135 g|flour
30 g|Sugar
½|egg(s), whisked
10 g|butter
50 g|sultanas
1 teaspoon|orange zest, grated
40 g|lemon peel
40 g|Orange peel
15 g|pistachios, chopped
½|egg(s), beaten
5 g|Chale sugar

Preparation

Warm the milk with the vanilla sugar until lukewarm and dissolve the yeast in it while stirring. Cover and leave in a warm place for 15 minutes. Meanwhile, put the flour in a bowl. Add 30 g sugar, 10 g butter in flakes, salt and ½ egg. Work everything into a smooth dough with the dough hook of the hand mixer and then with your hands. Cover again and leave to rise in a warm place for about 1 hour. Knead the dough again and knead in the orange zest and fruit, add a little more flour if necessary and place in a springform pan (12 cm diameter) lined with baking paper. If necessary, use baking parchment to make a higher edge. Leave the cake to rise for another 10 minutes, brush with the remaining egg and sprinkle with hail sugar. Then bake at 170 °C convection oven for about 35 minutes. Cover with aluminium foil if it browns too quickly.

PINE SIGHS

Total time approx.: 30 minutes

Ingredients

200 g|Pine kernels
200 g|Almond(s), without skin, ground
200 g|Sugar, fine
2 tablespoons|starch
1 teaspoon|lemon zest, grated
2|egg whites
1 pinch(s)|salt

Preparation

Coarsely chop 100 g pine nuts. Roast the chopped pine nuts and the almonds briefly without fat, stirring. Be careful not to burn anything! Leave the kernels to cool and then mix with sugar, cornflour and lemon zest. Beat the egg whites with salt until semi-stiff and fold in the pine nut and almond mixture. Using a teaspoon, scoop out walnut-sized heaps and place them a little apart on baking trays lined with baking paper. Press approx. 2-3 unroasted pine nuts into each mound. Place the trays in the oven preheated to 175°C (convection oven 160°C) (middle shelf) and bake for approx. 10 minutes. Remove the pine sighs with the baking paper from the tray and leave to cool. When cool, carefully remove from the baking paper.

PIGNOLI CROISSANTS

Total time approx.: 30 minutes

Ingredients

220 g|flour
¼ teaspoon|mace, (fresh)
1 pinch(s)|salt
150 g|Butter, softened
100 g|Sugar, brown
2|Yolk
1 tablespoon|orange(s) zest
1 packet|vanilla sugar
2 tablespoons|honey
60 g|Pine kernels

Preparation

Mix the flour, nutmeg and salt together and set aside. Heat the oven to 175 degrees C; grease two baking sheets. Beat the butter and brown sugar until fluffy. Add the egg yolks one at a time, then beat the mixture until firm. Add the orange zest and vanilla and mix well. Gradually add the flour mixture, beating well in between each addition. Use about 1 tablespoon per croissant, make a roll 3.5-cm long and then shape into a croissant; place about 5-cm apart on the prepared trays. Warm the honey slightly, just until it is runny and slightly warm; brush it lightly over the tops and sides of the croissants, then sprinkle generously with the nuts, pressing down lightly. Bake until the croissants are golden brown, about 10-12 minutes. Leave to cool on the tray for 1-2 minutes, then transfer to wire racks to cool completely.

ESPRESSO BISCUITS WITH CHOCOLATE FILLING

Total time approx.: 1 hour 5 minutes

Ingredients

100 g|Sweet chocolate
50 g|Powdered sugar
100 g|Butter
1|Yolk
40 ml|espresso, hot
200 g|flour
50 g|chocolate, plain
possibly|coffee beans, to garnish

Preparation

Break the chocolate into pieces and melt slowly in a hot water bath while stirring. In a mixing bowl, beat the icing sugar and butter with a hand mixer until creamy and stir in the egg yolks. Gradually mix in the espresso and chocolate. Add the sifted flour and knead into a smooth dough. Then wrap in cling film and leave to rest in the fridge for approx. 30 minutes. Roll out the dough between 2 layers of cling film with a rolling pin until it is 5 mm thin and cut into even, narrow rectangles. Line a baking tray with baking paper and then place the rectangles on it. Bake the pastry in a preheated oven at 180 degrees for 12-15 minutes. Then remove from the tray with the paper and leave to cool. Roughly chop the chocolate coating and melt it slowly over a bain-marie. Spread three quarters of the chocolate on half of the biscuits. Place the remaining biscuits on top. Using a piping bag, pipe the remaining chocolate coating in fine lines onto the biscuits. Decorate with coffee beans as desired.

AMARETTINI INSULANI STYLE

Total time approx.: 30 minutes

Ingredients

300 g|Almond(s), (peeled & ground)
8 drops|bitter almond flavouring, (as alcohol substitute)
300 g|Sugar
3|egg whites, (beat until stiff)
1 pinch(s) salt
100 g|powdered sugar, (for sprinkling)

Preparation

Mix the almonds, sugar and bitter almond oil and gently fold into the beaten egg whites. The dough should not be too soft. Roll into nut-sized balls and place on the baking tray lined with baking paper (8-tung! leave enough space between the biscuits!) Then bake in the middle of the oven preheated to 160° C for 30 minutes. Sprinkle with icing sugar while still warm and leave to cool. Remove from the paper only after they have cooled.

BACI D`AMORE

Total time approx.: 30 minutes

Ingredients

175 g|Butter
175 g|Powdered sugar
1 pinch(s) salt
3|egg(s)
250 g|flour
40 g|cocoa powder
150 g|chocolate, plain
100 g|cream
150 g|marzipan paste
|icing sugar

Preparation

Cream butter, icing sugar, salt. Beat in the eggs, then stir in
the flour and cocoa powder. Fill the dough into a piping bag
with a nozzle and pipe cat tongues approx. 5cm long. Bake in
the oven at 180° for approx. 10 min. Then leave to cool. For
the filling, roughly chop the chocolate. Bring the cream to the
boil and dissolve the chocolate in it. Leave to cool until it is
still spreadable. Spread the chocolate cream on the underside
of half of the biscuits and place the remaining biscuits on top.
Chill. Roll thin strands of the marzipan paste and wrap them
in a bow around the biscuits and dust with icing sugar.

MOCHA PANFORTE

Total time approx.: 13 hours 5 minutes

Ingredients

200 ml|coffee
100 ml|liqueur, (coffee liqueur)
200 g|Fruits, dried (e.g. apricots, apples)
100 g|Sugar
175 g|Honey
100 g|Butter
100 g|Fig(s), dried
250 g|flour
50 g|cocoa powder, plus cocoa for dusting
1 tablespoon|coffee powder, soluble
½ teaspoon|cinnamon
1 pinch|of clove(s)
1 pinch|of nutmeg, freshly grated
1|Orange(s), organic, grated peel
70 g|hazelnuts
70 g|walnuts
70 g|Almond(s)

Preparation

Mix the coffee and liqueur. Soak the dried fruit (except figs) in it overnight. Drain and collect the liquid. Chop the fruit. Preheat the oven to 160 degrees (fan oven 140 degrees). Heat the sugar, honey, butter and the chopped dried fruit in a pan until the sugar has dissolved. Chop the figs into small pieces. Mix the flour, cocoa, coffee powder and spices and stir into the honey-fruit mixture together with the orange zest, all the nuts and almonds, the chopped figs. If the mixture is too firm, stir in about 100 ml soaking liquid. The dough should be sticky, not completely dry. Line a springform pan with baking paper, pour in the mixture and smooth it out. Bake in a hot oven for about 20 minutes. Leave to cool in the tin. Then take out, remove the baking paper and cut the cake into thin strips. Dust with cocoa powder.

FLORENTINE

Total time approx.: 50 minutes

Ingredients

100 g|Butter
80 g|Sugar
1 tablespoon|honey
2 tablespoons|condensed milk
2 tablespoons|flour
100 g|almond(s), sliced
2 tablespoons|currant or sultanas or chopped candied
orange peel or lemon peel, according to taste
100 g|chocolate, plain
|cherry(s) (cherries, to taste)

Preparation

Put the butter, sugar, honey, tinned milk and flour in a saucepan
and bring to the boil over a medium heat, stirring constantly.
Remove the pan from the heat, stir in the flaked almonds and
candied orange peel (or other) and leave the mixture to cool.
Preheat the oven to 190 degrees. Line a baking tray with baking
paper coated on both sides. Using a wet teaspoon, place small
mounds of dough on the tray, not too thick as the mixture
will melt. Bake the Florentines in the oven on the middle shelf
for about 10 minutes. Leave the biscuits to cool slightly on
the tray, then lift them down with a wide knife. Dissolve the
baking chocolate in a hot water bath (not above 40 degrees,
otherwise the chocolate will turn grey), brush the underside
of the Florentines with it and leave to dry well. If necessary,

stick a cherry on the front with a dab of chocolate coating.

GINGERBREAD CANTUCCINI

Total time approx.: 1 hour 33 minutes

Ingredients

250 g|Wheat flour
1 teaspoon|baking powder
2 teaspoons|gingerbread spice
175 g|sugar
1 bag/s|vanilla sugar
1 pinch(s)|salt
2|egg(s), size M
25 g|Butter, soft
35 g|Pistachio kernels, whole
35 g|Pistachio kernels, chopped
90 g|Cranberries, dried
|Flour for the work surface

Preparation

Mix the flour, baking powder, sugar, vanilla sugar, salt and gingerbread spice in a bowl. Beat the eggs and add to the flour mixture with the butter in flakes. Knead to a smooth dough and finally mix in the pistachios and cranberries - first electric, then reshape with your hands, it takes a little time. Wrap the dough in foil and place in the fridge for 30 minutes. Preheat the oven to 175 °C top/bottom heat. Divide the dough into quarters and shape each piece into a 4 cm diameter roll on a floured work surface. Place the 4 rolls spaced apart on a baking tray lined with baking paper and flatten slightly by hand. Bake the rolls for 15 minutes. Then leave to cool. Cut each roll diagonally into 0.5 cm thin slices. Place them with the cut side close together on two trays lined with baking paper and bake one after the other in a 175 °C oven for another 9 minutes. Leave the cantuccini to cool and store in an airtight tin.

POPPY SEED - AMARETTO - PANETTONE

Total time approx.: 1 hour 40 minutes

Ingredients

60 g|butter
1 tablespoon|butter
125 ml|milk
½ cube|yeast
2 tablespoons|sugar
350 g|flour
1 pinch(s) of salt
3|egg(s) (size M)
500 g| poppy seed cake
60 g|pine kernels
1 tablespoon|pine nuts
6 tablespoons|amaretto
|grease for the mould
|flour for the work surface

Preparation

First of all: If you don't have a panettone dish, you can simply use a springform pan and then increase the height of the pan by lining it with baking paper once around the inside. Melt the butter and leave to cool. Warm the milk to lukewarm and dissolve the yeast with the 1 tablespoon sugar in it. Put the sifted flour, salt and two eggs in a bowl. Add the milk mixture and butter and work into a smooth dough. If the dough still sticks too much, just add a little more flour. Cover the dough with a kitchen towel and leave to rise in a warm place for about 1 hour. Mix the poppy seed dough with 1 egg, 60 g pine nuts and the amaretto. Roll out the dough on a floured work surface into a rectangle (35 cm x 40 cm) and spread the poppy seed mixture on it with a spoon. Roll up the dough from the long side. Place the roll in the greased tin and press the ends together well. Melt 1 tablespoon of butter and brush the dough with it. Then sprinkle with 1 tablespoon of sugar and 1 tablespoon of pine nuts. Cover the panettone and let it rise for another 10 minutes. During this time, preheat the oven to 200°C top/bottom heat. Depending on the oven, the panettone will take about 40 minutes to bake. As the pine nuts burn easily, it is advisable to cover the panettone with aluminium foil as soon as it has taken on a nice colour (after about 30 minutes). Leave the panettone to rest in the tin for 10 minutes, then remove from the tin and leave to cool on a wire rack. And if you don't want to wait until it has cooled down: Personally, it tastes best even lukewarm.

PANFORTE

Total time approx.: 45 minutes

Ingredients

200 g|Hazelnuts
100 g|Walnuts
300 g|Almond(s)
150 g|Fig(s), dried
300 g|Fruits, candied, mixed
1 pinch(s)|pepper, white
1 pinch(s) nutmeg
150 g|Honey
150 g|powdered sugar
60 ml|water
|powdered sugar, for sprinkling

Preparation

Toast the nuts one by one in a dry pan, stirring constantly. Then leave to cool and chop coarsely. Cut the figs and candied fruit into small cubes and mix with the nuts and spices. Melt the honey with the icing sugar in a bain-marie. Carefully fold the nut-fruit mixture into the liquid honey. Add water little by little until the mixture binds. Pour everything into a springform pan lined with baking paper and smooth out. Bake in the preheated oven at 150°C for about 30 minutes. Dust with icing sugar.

CHRISTMAS CANTUCCINI

Total time approx.: 35 minutes

Ingredients

500 g|flour
1 teaspoon|baking powder
3 large|egg(s)
250 g|sugar
2 teaspoons|cinnamon powder
2 teaspoons|clove powder
2 teaspoons|orange zest, grated
2 teaspoons|lemon zest, grated
2 tablespoons|amaretto
50 g|butter
30 g|butter fat
200 g|walnuts

Preparation

Mix flour with baking powder and sift into a bowl. Beat the eggs. Add all ingredients except the nuts to the flour bowl. Knead thoroughly with the dough hook of the hand mixer. Then, on a floured work surface, knead the dough with your hands until smooth, incorporating the walnuts. Divide the dough into four equal portions and form each into rolls that still fit on the baking tray. Line the baking tray with baking paper, place the rolls on it and bake at 180°C (fan oven 160°C) on the middle shelf for about 45 minutes. Leave the dough rolls to rest for 5 minutes after baking, then cut diagonally into slices approx. 2 cm thick.

DARK PRINTEN - CANTUCCHINI WITH CASHEW AND WALNUTS

Total time approx.: 30 minutes

Ingredients

260 g|flour
1 teaspoon|baking powder
2 teaspoons|cocoa powder
35 g|Butter, soft
2|egg(s)
1 pinch(s) salt
2 teaspoons|spice mix, (speculaas spice)
75 g|Cashew nuts, can also be lightly salted
75 g|walnuts, halves again
|cashew nuts, can also be lightly salted

Preparation

Knead all the ingredients, except the nuts, into a dough. Only then work in the nuts, which requires some tact and patience, as the nuts sometimes try to get out of the dough. Then carefully form 2 sausages of the same size so that they fit lengthwise on the baking tray. Bake these 2 "sausages" at 190°C for 18-20 minutes. Take them out and let them rest for about 5 minutes.

In the meantime, turn down the oven to 180°C. Now cut the "sausages" diagonally with a VERY sharp knife into slices about 1 1/2 cm thick and bake again for 12-15 minutes.

RAFFAELLO

Total time approx.: 1 day 40 minutes

Ingredients

200 ml|water
400 g|Sugar
100 g|milk powder (already available in every supermarket)
200 g|Coconut flakes
250 g|Butter
200 g|hazelnuts, peeled, (if possible)
200 g|Coconut flakes, for rolling

Preparation

Melt sugar in water over low heat, stirring constantly. Remove the pan from the heat and melt the butter. Stir in 200 g coconut flakes, then add the powdered milk. Leave the mixture to cool and refrigerate for 24 hours. The next day, shape the dough into small balls, press a peeled hazelnut into each ball, roll the balls in the coconut flakes and place them in paper moulds.

BAKED FIGS WRAPPED WITH PROSCIUTTO IN GORGONZOLA SAUCE

Total time approx.: 30 minutes

Ingredients

4|Fig(s)
4 slice/s|ham, (prosciutto)
½ teaspoon|butter
100 ml|cream
150 g|Gorgonzola

Preparation

Wrap 1 slice of prosciutto around 1 fig, pin tightly with toothpicks and place in an ovenproof dish. Melt some butter in a pan/small saucepan, add the Gorgonzola and pour the cream on top. Melt slowly over a low heat, leave to cool a little, then it will thicken a little more and spoon over the figs. Cover the dish with aluminium foil and bake in a preheated oven at approx. 180°C for 10 minutes. Remove the foil and bake for another 1-3 minutes. Place 2 figs per portion on a plate, remove toothpick and spoon sauce over. Serve 2 figs per portion as a starter, but with a salad and baguette it also makes a good main course!

CHRISTMAS CROSTINI FROM PUGLIA

Total time approx.: 20 minutes

Ingredients

8 slice/s|white bread, thin
40 g|Gorgonzola
25 g|Butter, unsalted
25 g|Walnuts
2 teaspoons|whisky or brandy

Preparation

Preheat the oven to 180 degrees. Cut the bread into Christmas motifs using cookie cutters, brush with olive oil and toast in the oven. In a saucepan, mix the Gorgonzola, butter and whisky over a moderate heat. Stir in half of the walnuts and spread on the crostinis after mixing thoroughly. Garnish with the remaining walnuts.

MILANESE

Total time approx.: 30 minutes

Ingredients

50 g|Palm fat
75 g|butter fat or goat butter
100 g|sugar
1 small|egg(s)
|vanilla sugar
200 g|flour
50 g|corn starch
possibly|egg yolk to coat

Preparation

Knead a dough from all the ingredients. Roll out between two sheets of plastic wrap and either cut out different shapes or shape as desired. Brush with an egg yolk, depending on your mood. Bake at 170°C for about 10 to 15 minutes until golden.

PANE DEGLI ANGELI

Total time approx.: 15 minutes

Ingredients

200 g|Butter
200 g|Sugar
1 packet|vanilla sugar
3|egg(s)
250 g|cooking starch
3 teaspoons|baking powder
½|lemon(s), untreated, zest grated
|margarine, for greasing

Preparation

Baking time: 25 minutes Electric oven 220 degrees, gas mark 3 or 1/3 high flame, fan oven 200 degrees Cream the butter, sugar and vanilla sugar until light and fluffy. Gradually stir in the eggs and lemon zest. Mix the cornflour and baking powder and fold in. Pour the batter into a greased springform pan (diameter 26 cm). Place in the preheated oven on the lowest shelf. After 15 minutes, cover with parchment paper. After a total baking time of 25 minutes, remove from the oven and leave to cool in the tin for 10 minutes, remove from the tin and cut into 12 pieces.

ITALIAN ANISEED COOKIES

Total time approx.: 1 day 30 minutes

Ingredients

250 g|flour
5 g|Baking powder
250 g|Sugar
1 tablespoon|cherry water
1 tablespoon|aniseed, lightly crushed
15 g|Butter

Preparation

Beat the eggs with the sugar and butter in a bowl until creamy. Gradually add the flour, baking powder, cherry brandy and aniseed and mix well. Line a baking tray with baking paper. Use a spoon to place small mounds of dough on the tray. Leave to rest in a cool place for 24 hours. Bake in the oven preheated to 180°C for approx. 20 minutes.

HONEY PLAITS

Total time approx.: 55 minutes

Ingredients

350 g|flour (pasta flour)
250 g|Butter
100 g|Sugar
4|Yolk
140 g|honey
1 package|vanilla sugar
½ teaspoon|gingerbread spice
1 pinch(s)|salt

Preparation

Mix the butter, sugar and vanilla sugar. Mix in 100 g honey and 3 egg yolks. Mix flour, salt and gingerbread spice and knead in. Cover the dough and chill for 1 hour. Preheat the oven to 200 degrees. Take pieces of the dough about the size of a walnut and roll out into ropes about 20 cm long. Fold the strands in half and braid into plaits. Whisk the remaining honey with 1 egg yolk and brush the honey plaits with it. Bake the biscuits for about 15 minutes.

PINE BISCUITS

Total time approx.: 30 minutes

Ingredients

2|egg(s), (of which the white for snow)
1 pinch(s) salt
150 g|pine nuts
125 g|sugar
½|lemon(s), of which the zest

Preparation

Beat the egg whites with the salt until very stiff. Finely grind 100 g pine nuts and mix with the sugar and lemon zest and add by the spoonful to the egg white mixture, beating constantly.Roughly chop the remaining pine nuts and add to the egg white mixture. Preheat the oven to 120° and place small heaps on a greased baking tray (you can also use wafers). Bake the pine biscuits on the middle shelf for about 50 minutes, leave to cool on a cooling rack and seal airtight.

ALMOND BREAD BISCUITS

Total time approx.: 40 minutes

Ingredients

200 g|Almond(s), peeled
400 g|flour
1 pinch(s) salt
300 g|Sugar
3|egg(s)
2|egg(s), of which the yolk(s)
1 tablespoon|baking powder
1 pinch(s) saffron
|milk

Preparation

Lightly roast the almonds without fat. Sieve the flour into a bowl, make a well in the middle and add the salt, sugar, eggs and 1 egg yolk, saffron and baking powder. Knead all the ingredients into a smooth dough, adding a little milk if necessary if the dough becomes too firm. Only knead in the almonds at the end. Preheat the oven to 175°, grease the baking tray and dust with flour. Roll the dough into 5 cm long, 1 cm thick sticks, place them on the baking tray, brush with the egg yolk and bake for about 30 minutes until light yellow. Remove from the baking tray and cut into diagonal pieces, place on a cooling rack and leave to dry, lightly sugar and store in a tin that can be easily closed. Keeps well for a long time. In Tuscany they dip them in Vin Santo.

GOLOSI

Total time approx.: 2 hours 40 minutes

Ingredients

405 g|flour
195 g|sugar
1 tablespoon|honey
250 g|butter
1 package|yeast (dry yeast)
1 packet|chocolate (chocolate buttons, baking ingredients
or 125 g cooking chocolate), roughly chopped
|powdered sugar, for dusting

Preparation

Knead all the ingredients quickly into a dough and chill
in the KS for at least 2 hours. Then roll out the dough
and cut out round biscuits. Bake at 180° for about 10
minutes until golden. Dust with icing sugar.

RICE BISCUITS

Total time approx.: 30 minutes

Ingredients

1 litre|milk
150 g|sugar
1 pinch(s) salt
300 g|milk rice
4|egg(s)
100 g|flour
1|orange(s), untreated, of which the zest is removed
2 tablespoons|baking powder
|olive oil, for frying
|sugar and cinnamon powder for sprinkling

Preparation

Boil the milk with the sugar and salt, sprinkle in the rice and cook it for about 40 minutes until soft, (let it steam) cool. Then add the eggs, flour and orange peel with the baking powder and mix well. Heat enough olive oil in a saucepan to bake the biscuits in it until they are floating. Flatten the rice mixture with a tablespoon and fry in the hot olive oil until golden brown, immediately drain on kitchen paper, mix the sugar with the cinnamon and roll the biscuits in it.

PANETTONE WITH PINE NUTS, CHOCOLATE AND CRANBERRIES

Total time approx.: 3 hours 5 minutes

Ingredients

200 ml|milk, lukewarm
½ cube|yeast, fresh
100 g|sugar
500 g|flour
2|vanilla pod(s), the pith of it
1 pinch|sea salt
2|egg yolks
100 g|butter, soft
1 teaspoon|lemon zest
60 g|Pine kernels
80 g|chocolate chips, plain
60 g|cranberries
1 tablespoon|butter for spreading

Preparation

Warm the milk, pour into a mixing bowl, crumble in the yeast and add 20 g of the sugar. Mix well and let the yeast work for 10 - 15 minutes. Now put all the remaining ingredients for the dough into a bowl and knead well together, cover with a damp cloth and leave in a warm place for about 1.5 hours or longer until doubled in volume. Knead the pine nuts, chocolate chips and cranberries into the dough, place the dough in a greased or paper baking tin and leave to rise again for 30 - 40 minutes, covered in a warm place. Cut the dough crosswise on the surface with a sharp knife or a carpet knife. This takes the tension out of the dough. Pour half a cup of water into the Airfryer. Place the baking tin in the cold Airfryer and bake at 150 °C convection oven for approx. 20 minutes. After 5 - 10 minutes, brush the surface with a little butter and bake until done. Remove from the tin and leave to cool on a cooling rack.

BRUTTI MA BUONI

Total time approx.: 1 hour 20 minutes

Ingredients

100 g|Hazelnuts
100 g|Almond(s)
1 teaspoon|cinnamon powder
2|egg whites
1 pinch(s) salt
90 g|cane sugar
1|lemon(s), zest and juice thereof
1 pinch|vanilla pod(s), ground

Preparation

Place the whole nuts on a baking tray and roast at 200 °C top/bottom heat for about 10 minutes. Leave the kernels to cool slightly and rub a few nuts against each other between your hands to loosen the shell. Pour boiling water over the almonds, leave to stand for five minutes and then peel off the skin, e.g. let it snap between your fingers. Roughly chop the nuts and almonds and roast them in a pan with the cinnamon until it starts to smell. Let everything cool down a little. Beat the egg whites with a pinch of salt until stiff. Add the sugar, lemon zest and juice and continue beating until the sugar has dissolved. Add the foam mixture to the roasted nuts and almonds. Add the ground vanilla and warm everything up to about 40 degrees while stirring. When the mixture has cooled a little, place small heaps on a baking tray lined with foil or paper (approx. 60 pieces) and bake at 150 °C convection oven for approx.

10 - 15 minutes until they start to colour. Leave the biscuits to cool on the tray and then layer them in a suitable tin.

MILAN BAY LEAVES

Total time approx.: 42 minutes

Ingredients

300 g|flour
60 g|Sugar
1 pinch(s)|salt
½|lemon(s), grated zest of it only
30 g|butter
6|egg yolks
|flour for the work surface
2|egg whites for brushing

Preparation

Sieve the flour, mix with the sugar, salt and lemon zest. Allow the butter to become liquid, whisk with the egg yolks and incorporate, adding a little more milk if necessary. Roll out on a lightly floured work surface to a thickness of approx. 0.5 cm and cut out biscuits in the shape of bay leaves (or other leaves). Press in the typical leaf structure with the back of a knife. Brush with egg white to give the finished bay leaves a nice shine. Baking heat: preheated to 200 °C top/bottom heat, 180 °C convection oven, gas: level 3 Baking time: a good 12 minutes The bay leaves must be golden yellow, but may be brown around the edges and at the tips. Storage: In a tightly closing tin.

BRAISED EEL WITH SAVOY CABBAGE

Total time approx.: 1 hour 25 minutes

Ingredients

1 medium|sized eel(s), green, i.e. not smoked, approx. 400 g
½ head|mullet
¼ packet|butter, approx. 125 g
½ small|onion(s)
½|carrot(s)
½ can|tomatoes, chunky
100 ml|white wine, dry
1|leaf of bay leaf
|salt and pepper
2 tablespoons|pine nuts

Preparation

Cut the savoy half into 2 parts and separate the leaves one by one. Cut the large leaves in half again if necessary, wash if necessary. Finely chop the onion and carrots and fry them in the heated butter in a deep pan, then deglaze with wine and reduce a little. Add the tomatoes and bay leaf. Season with salt and pepper and simmer on a low heat with a lid for about 20 minutes. Add the savoy cabbage and simmer for another 20 minutes with the lid on. Then add the eel to the pot and simmer again with the lid on for about 20 minutes (or longer), stirring the stew gently from time to time. Before serving, sprinkle the dish with the roasted pine nuts.

ROAST PORK WITH MUSHROOMS

Total time approx.: 2 hours 10 minutes

Ingredients

800 g|Roast pork without rind
15 g|boletus mushrooms, dried
1 sprig/s|rosemary, fresh, approx. 10 cm
long or 20 rosemary needles
4|sage leaves
1 pinch(s) thyme
1 pinch(s) of marjoram
2|clove(s) of garlic
6 tablespoons|olive oil, extra virgin, cold pressed
100 ml|red wine
100 ml|cream
|salt
|pepper, black

Preparation

Soak the porcini mushrooms in 100 ml water in a cup. Put 3 tablespoons of olive oil in a bowl with just enough room for the meat. Chop the sage leaves and mix with the rosemary, thyme, marjoram and oil. Put the roast in and marinate for 1/2 hour. Turn the meat from time to time. Heat 3 tablespoons of olive oil in a pot over medium heat and brown the garlic cloves and the roast pork with the marinade on all sides. Deglaze with red wine. Chop the mushrooms and add them with the soaking water.

Season with salt and pepper and, depending on the quality of the meat, leave to braise for about 1.5 hours at a low temperature, covered. Add a little water if necessary. Remove the meat, cut into thin slices and arrange on a platter. Stir the cream into the sauce, bring to the boil briefly and pour the sauce over the meat. Serve with patate sabbiose or potatoes from the oven mixed with breadcrumbs and seasoned with garlic, sage and rosemary.

TIRAMISU NATALE

Total time approx.: 18 hours 40 minutes

Ingredients

65 g|Sugar
3|egg(s)
50 g|marzipan
100 ml|liqueur (cappuccino liqueur)
250 g|Mascarpone
100 ml|cream
200 g|sponge fingers
3 dashes|bitter almond flavouring
|cocoa powder for baking

Preparation

Cream together the sugar, egg yolks and marzipan (I used some with a dark coating). Add the mascarpone, whipped cream and stiffly beaten egg whites. Drizzle in the bitter almond flavouring. Drizzle the ladyfingers with the liqueur and layer half of them in a mould. Cover with half of the cream and place the remaining sponge fingers on top. Finally, cover with the remaining cream and dust with cocoa. Leave in the fridge for one night.

FIG CONFECTION

Total time approx.: 30 minutes

Ingredients

80 g|Almond(s), unpeeled
400 g|Fig(s), large dried ones
40 g|citron
1 teaspoon|clove(s), ground
200 g|chocolate (block chocolate, household chocolate)
50 ml|water
1 tablespoon|sugar

Preparation

Roast the almonds without fat, always turning them. Remove the hard end pieces from the figs and cut them in the middle, place two almonds, some candied lemon peel, some clove powder in the pocket and press them well shut, place them on a lightly greased baking tray and put them in the oven for about 15 minutes at medium heat, they should only colour slightly. Meanwhile, melt the chocolate with a little water and a spoonful of sugar. Put the stuffed figs on a wooden skewer and drag them through the chocolate mixture. They should be covered all around. Let them dry on a cake rack, put them into paper moulds and store them in a tin. (without skewers)

CAPPUCCINO DREAMS

Total time approx.: 2 hours

Ingredients

50 g|Chocolate, diced (1/2 cm) Espresso cream or mocha cream
100 g|Butter, room temperature
100 g|Powdered sugar
|salt
3 tablespoons|coffee powder (espresso), soluble
2|egg(s), 1 separated
150 g|flour
½ teaspoon|baking powder
50 g|hazelnuts, ground
3 tablespoons|coffee, cold
30 g|Sugar

Preparation

You need 50 praline moulds. Cream the fat, icing sugar and 1 pinch of salt and the espresso powder for at least 5 minutes. Stir in the egg and egg yolk. Sieve the flour and baking powder and fold in with the coffee and nuts. Place the ramekins on baking trays. Use a piping bag with a nozzle to pipe the batter into the moulds and press a chocolate cube into the centre of each. Bake in the preheated oven at 180 degrees for 9 minutes. Beat the egg whites with a pinch of salt until stiff, add the sugar and continue to beat for 3 minutes. Using a piping bag with a small nozzle, pipe the egg white mixture onto the pre-baked cupcakes. Bake for a further 5-6 minutes and then leave to cool.

SPICY CHOCOLATE TARTUFI

Total time approx.: 4 hours 25 minutes

Ingredients

200 g|Cream
250 g|Dark chocolate, 70%
1 tablespoon|butter
1 pinch(s)|sea salt, (fleur de sel)
1 dash|rum
some|cocoa powder
1 pinch(s) nutmeg, ground
1 pinch(s) ginger, ground
1 pinch(s)|pepper, ground
a few|paper cups

Preparation

Heat the cream in a saucepan. Roughly chop the chocolate and melt it in the cream. Add the butter, salt and rum and stir in. Put the mixture in the fridge for at least 3 hours. The mixture must be firm. Use a spoon to cut off small pieces of the mixture and form into balls. Place the balls in the fridge for 1 hour. In the meantime, put the cocoa, nutmeg, ginger and pepper on a plate and mix. Remove the firm balls from the fridge and roll them in the cocoa mixture. Place the finished tartufi in paper moulds and store in an airtight container in the fridge.

IMPRINT

We help you to publish your book!

By

TTENTION Inc.
Wilmington - DE19806
Trolley Square 20c

Instagram: mindful_publishing
Contact: mindful.publishing@web.de

Printed in Great Britain
by Amazon

35261848R00050